MW01630980

What People Are Saying

"As a mentor to more than 150 agents worldwide, I'm always looking for a way to give my people an edge out in the field. Mike's book is more than a good read. It's a great tool, but only if you're serious about your success."

Sol Hicks, Top of the Table Member and Speaker, United States

"Sometimes the simpler a concept is, the more impact it will have. Mike has the ability to take complex situations and present them so simply that everybody gets it, and that includes the advisor, the client, or the professional contact you are trying to develop. Mike Morrow really is the advisors' Advisor."

Doug Bennett, DipPFS MDRT member of 8 years with one COT qualification, England

"Mike's enthusiasm for going out of his way to deliver service to his clients and share that knowledge and experience with others is amazing. He is one of the most passionate people in this area I know, and having seen him speak several times, this is extremely evident, and the time you are with him never seems long enough. Several of Mike's ideas have been developed and put to immediate good use within my own practice."

David Braithwaite,
DipPFS Managing Director,
Citrus Financial, England

"Mike Morrow knows what the media wants — honest, tell-it-like-it-is commentary that explains what complex events mean to everyday investors."

Rob Carrick,
Personal Finance Columnist,
The Globe and Mail, Canada

"Mike brings a wealth of knowledge about how to help advisors grow their business. He delivers the material with enthusiasm, humor, and encouragement to become a better advisor."

Robert Gignac, Author,
Rich Is A State of Mind, Canada

"In Mike Morrow you have a lot of very simple subtle humor that reveals some very powerful truths about being a financial advisor in this world. You just gotta love him."

Jim Ruta, AdvisorCraft, Canada

"Your book is so easy to follow. Your ideas are amazing. I am using your strategies to better serve my clients. Thank you."

Aurora Tancock CFP,
Aurora Tancock Financial
Services Inc., Canada

"I've been in the business for thirty years, and Mike Morrow brought a very refreshing approach that I'm definitely going to benefit from, and in the long run, my clients will definitely benefit from. It was great, one of the best sales conferences I've been to in years."

Greg Bowen, CFP CLU CH.F.C.

"What I really enjoyed about hearing Mike Morrow today is the value that I can take and use with my clients. This has been a phenomenal opportunity to see something that can help you grow."

Mike Stewart, CFP CLU CH.F.C.,
Canada

THE LOYALTY EDGE

Proven strategies to foster client loyalty

Mike Morrow, CFP

The Loyalty Edge

by Mike Morrow, CFP

200-905 Tungsten St.
Thunder Bay, ON, Canada P7B 5Z3
Phone 1-807-684-1805
Toll Free 1-877-684-1805
mike@ideasforadvisors.com
www.ideasforadvisors.com

Development: Michelle Brown,
michelle.brown.solutions@gmail.com

Cover and interior design: Carla Green,
carla@studiocgraphics.com

Published by Ideas for Advisors LLC

ISBN: 978-0-9940846-0-6

Contents

Foreword

I have known Mike for over ten years. I have been impressed with how he has always been a student of the business. He surrounds himself with successful people. He networks at industry meetings better than anyone I know. I've had the pleasure of attending a number of events with Mike, including numerous NAIFA and MDRT events. He is a passionate and humorous speaker who gives simple and practical ways for advisors to increase their production and more importantly to better protect their clients.

In his new book, *The Loyalty Edge*, Mike's vigorous personality and underlying sense of humor jump right off the pages and resonate with his readers as if he was speaking on stage in front of a crowded room. His energy is high and his goal is simple: Let me take your business to the next level!

When it comes to educating yourself on how to build your book of business and attract new prospects, there are a million and one products out there to choose from! They all claim they have the "best strategies" or the "best formulas" or the "best ideas" in the business. Well, as great as that sounds, are they going to guarantee a line of new prospects at your office door? I don't think so. Continuous education is necessary when growing your book of business. How else are you going to learn the tricks of the trade? Read. Attend seminars. Read. Invest in online training tools. Read. Listen to audiobooks like the Kinder Brothers, who made a huge impact on my life and got me to where I am today (I'll never forget those dusty

VHS tapes for as long as I live!) And, read! There is so much useful information out there, you just need to go out there and find it.

Now, a lot of the educational products we see today give good advice on how to build your brand, gain new prospects, and teach you how to stand out from the rest. A lot of books and products are fluffed up with fancy diagrams and elaborate formulas. What they are missing is the passion. In this industry, you have to find the passionate ones. I believe that Mike Morrow is truly one of the passionate ones!

Both Mike and I look at the math and science that goes into each scenario. No fluff. He takes the millions of strategies and formulas that we see on a day-to-day basis, finds the ones that work, and simplifies them so that they make sense. His simple, back to basics approach makes his formulas easy to follow so that you can utilize them in your own ways. The everyday aspects of life can already seem complicated enough at times that when it comes to learning the necessary steps to take to build your brand, who doesn't want the fastest, easiest, and most logical approach? Mike eases advisors as they take those fundamental steps! Hence, his EASE Formula for Success! Check it out as well as his other practical formulas that have been proven to increase effectiveness and boost sales efficiency!

From handwritten cards to historic newspapers, concept calendars, and a powerful way to deliver policies, Mike shares ways you can stand out. I know for a fact that Mike implements these strategies in his own practice! He KNOWS they work. They are simple and any advisor can do them. This book is loaded with many other strategies to meet people, build trust and loyalty and retain these clients forever! Combine this with his previous book, *The Picture Sells the Story*, and I believe you have everything you need to succeed in this business.

When it comes to Mike, one thing that I will tell you is that he is all about client appreciation. He views clients not as prospects, but as advocates of his brand. How do your clients get from prospects to advocates? Simple — by creating personal relationships, building that trust and loyalty, and being passionate about your brand.

Today, when it comes to seeking financial advice, many people are reluctant. Talking about finances, retirement, life insurance, etc. can feel very daunting and overwhelming to people. You need to make them feel special, safe, and secure from the minute they sit down to the minute they leave your office. Following up with a personalized note, lunch on the business, or catching up over a cup of coffee makes you stand out among the rest. These are all examples of how to create personal relationships with your clients that Mike discusses in this book.

For those of you who have had the pleasure of seeing Mike in action up on stage in front of a crowd, when it comes to this book, you know what you are in store for. For those who may not be familiar with Mike, brace yourselves and take a lot of notes!

— Tom Hegna, www.retirehappynow.com

Preface

We wrote this book to help busy advisors improve their overall results and effectiveness in this business. As a practicing advisor myself, I understand the need for simple strategies that make a difference; tools and strategies that we can pick up, touch, hold, feel and use right away to help grow our business.

Although we write with financial advisors in mind, the truth is anyone in any type of service-oriented business will benefit by using these simple client loyalty strategies. These ideas work. We know that they work because we have used them to help grow our business and improve our client loyalty over the past 25 years. In addition, I have been fortunate to have been invited to speak at conferences and workshops all over the world. It is so gratifying when another financial advisor who has heard me speak or purchased one of our books, explains how they have used one of our ideas.

The Loyalty Edge is full of creative ideas that are designed to foster client loyalty and set you apart from other advisors. Incorporating our strategies will have a positive impact on your business. Having said that, we want to emphasize the importance of all the things that you have been doing up until now that have made you successful. You need to continue to keep in regular contact with your clients. Do a great job solving your client's goals. Provide your clients with a financial plan and great reporting. These things are extremely important to your success. Continue to go out for breakfast or lunch with clients. Build relationships with your clients. Remember what my friend Don Connelly has been saying for years, 'People will eventually fire their stock broker or financial planner, but it is much harder to fire a friend.'

We consider this book to be a collection of the best ideas we have come across over our 25 years in business. Some are our own ideas and others are simply tweaks to the tried and true basics that we all know. We strive to make these ideas easy to implement by providing all of the steps and any supporting documents: wording for cards and notes, resources etc.

We see this book as an evolution. We are constantly on the lookout for new strategies to improve our client loyalty. We are always striving to improve our systems. In turn we share them with you.

I would like to thank the people who worked so hard to complete this book. My partner in development is Michelle Brown. She runs the show for developing our client loyalty strategies. I come up with an idea and then send it to her and she puts it all together. We then implement it with our clients and if it works, we develop it further into a true turnkey strategy that other advisors can use with their clients. Heather Mulae is our incredible editor, and Carla Green (www.studiocgraphics.com) is responsible for our beautiful graphic design. They never let us down and their work is fantastic!

Much of my success has come from making the choice many years ago to join the Million Dollar Round Table, **www.mdrt.org**. I have many friends and mentors that I have met through MDRT who are so important to me. I want to thank them for their support and encouragement over the years. I feel that I do need to single out four gentlemen who inspire me to reach greater heights: Don Connelly, Tom Hegna, George Sigurdson, and Guy Baker. These four superstars have always been able to keep a log going under my fire. There are not enough words to thank them for all that they have done to help me over the years.

— Mike Morrow
April 18, 2015

Our goal is
to ignite your
creative energy with
easy-to-implement
ideas that will take
your business to the
next level.

INTRODUCTION

The Framework of Your Success

At Ideas for Advisors, we strive to provide you with actionable and innovative marketing strategies to help you improve client retention, attract new clients and ultimately increase your bottom line. Our goal is to ignite your creative energy with easy to implement ideas that will take your business to the next level, simplify the complicated and help you make a lasting impression. In developing our strategies, we worked to eliminate any obstacles that would prevent you from incorporating them into your practice.

In this book you will find:

- Strategies to stand out from all other advisors that shows credibility and professionalism
- Prospecting tips that will keep your name top-of-mind
- Ideas to show client appreciation
- Tools to help you better engage with clients
- Examples for easy implementation
- And much more!

If you are like me, you have boxes and boxes of really good ideas that you have never used. Magazine cutouts, conference handouts, workshop notes; burning ideas at the time, but somehow ended up in 'that box', with a label that reads: *A lot of really great ideas that*

I am never going to use. Our goal for this book is to NOT end up in that box. We took all of our successful tried and true strategies and put them into one easy to use book for you, complete with templates and guidelines that are necessary for success. If you feel pulled in 101 directions and feel that it's impossible to incorporate any new strategies, this book is for you.

We are providing the knowledge, but it is up to you to transform knowing into doing. Knowing means nothing without taking the knowledge and putting it to work for you. Our strategies are easy to do but also easy not to do. The choice becomes yours. Every day is a new opportunity to be a better version of you, and this book will help you learn new ways to add value to your clients. We hope our strategies make a positive difference in your business today and tomorrow.

THE THOUGHT PROCESS BEHIND THE STRATEGIES

Early on in my career, I realized I needed to do something that would make me stand out from every other advisor. I knew I had to build my brand, but more importantly I had to find ways to foster loyalty with my client base. I wanted to give my clients reasons to talk about me and to be able to answer the question, "Why do you do business with Mike?" I wanted their answer to be, "Because he cares about me." With a keen interest in marketing and a foundation of providing value to my clients, I developed a system of marketing strategies that are shared in this book.

The 200 Client Philosophy

I have always seen my clients as my pension plan. I regularly ask myself, how am I protecting this investment? How can I effectively foster loyalty with my client base? Recognizing that it is much easier to keep clients than to find new clients, I was determined to work really hard at keeping my clients happy.

I talk about the 200 client philosophy in my key notes. I believe this is a valuable exercise — I hope it motivates you to transform knowing into doing.

Imagine that you start you career as a financial advisor, and you are given 200 clients. Your annual income is $200,000. BUT you can never ever take on another client for the rest of your career. How would your behavior with your clients change? What would you do to protect this revenue? The only opportunity to grow your business is to get every possible revenue stream from your clients. Imagine what your business approach would be if the lifetime revenue stream of your business was your existing clients.

View Your Business as a Brand

Every business has a brand. If you disagree, consider this. Do you know an advisor who is always late getting to work or to an appointment? Unfortunately for them, being late is part of their brand. What is your brand with your clients? Would you like your clients to say: 'My Financial Advisor looks out for my best interest. We communicate regularly. He is genuine and one-of-a-kind'? Being a one-of-a-kind advisor, now that would be a great brand.

Marketing is part of your brand. In the pages ahead we will give you innovative, tangible marketing strategies. Using these ideas will improve your brand, and professional image. Ultimately make you and your clients more successful.

THE FRAMEWORK

EASE = Education Activity Skills Excitement

We made sure all of our marketing strategies could be implemented with EASE™ (education, activity, skills and excitement). Most advisors and clients want a life, less difficult and simplified. The EASE™ formula will help ensure that during the financial planning process.

EASE: (defin.) 1. To render less difficult
2. Freedom from labour and pain, anxiety; freedom from great effort; freedom from financial need

The EASE™ Formula for Success

E – Education: In each chapter, we strive to better educate you on how you can successfully implement our client appreciation strategies to increase your bottom line. You will learn how to effectively integrate our ideas into your business, and explore the expense of each marketing strategy. We encourage you to consider the lifetime value of a client and what it means to you and your business, when you are considering the expense. At the conclusion of each marketing strategy, we ask whether you feel the idea presented is an investment or an expense. Marketing is an investment to protect your greatest asset — your clients. If you keep your clients happy, you will be able to have a lifetime of long-term relationships.

We believe that a life of EASE™ is the ultimate goal for advisors and clients.

How much do you really know about your business? Do you know your numbers? What was your bottom last year? What was your client retention? Of the clients you lost, what revenue was lost?

Improving your client retention is the best way to improve your bottom line. To make this point we encourage you to review your client list from 3 years ago and compare it to your client list today — what names have disappeared and why?

Imagine, you are the steward of 200 households and 4% of them leave each year — that would mean that you would lose 8 households per year. What would your business look like in 10 years if 40% of your households had left you for another advisor? Achieving 96% retention each year may sound satisfactory but when you think of 96% retention year after year the dismal picture becomes very clear.

We teach compounding to our clients all the time. Compounding works in your business too. When you improve your retention by

2%, imagine how different your business would look in as little as 10 years. 20% different!

In order to improve your client retention you need to ask yourself, 'Why did they leave?' The #1 reason clients leave is lack of contact. We will give you ideas to reach out to clients in a way that will have your clients feeling excited about the services you offer.

Retaining clients is easier than attracting new clients.

A – Activity: A financial advisor's activities fall into three categories: running your business, attracting clients and retaining clients. Only two of these activities are revenue-generating activities: retaining clients and attracting clients. Your time allocation and activity needs to be based around those two factors. Running your business is essential, but we need to remind ourselves that we run a revenue-generating business and our time needs to be allocated. With our marketing strategies you will learn how to attract and retain clients.

Every marketing idea that we present to you is scored or measured against *The Marketing Strategy Criteria for Success Checklist:*

Marketing Strategy Criteria for Success

- ✔ **Does the information establish you as a credible source?**
- ✔ **Is it going to differentiate you from everyone else?**
- ✔ **Does it have high impact?**
- ✔ **Does it have long shelf life?**

The Results

Your efforts should fall into these four revenue generating areas. As a revenue generating business, you need to:

1. **Attract additional assets / insurance sales**
2. **Generate quality referrals**
3. **Improve your client retention**
4. **Demonstrate your value proposition**

Wake up every morning with the objective of making yourself better than you were the day before.

S – Skills: As an advisor, our goal is to solve our clients' financial problems and bring value to them and future generations. This is only possible if we effectively communicate financial messages to them. When your clients feel confident in your guidance, they will be moved to action. Our financial concepts are a powerful way to communicate financial concepts in easy to digest language that your clients will understand. Our messages are clear and compelling, which will help you increase client retention.

If you do not have the skill to move your clients to action, you will not be successful.

E – Excitement: We are all striving to be successful, and the secret to success is excitement. If you are excited about being in this business, then your clients will be excited. Our marketing strategies and financial concepts are designed to make and keep you and your clients excited about the products and services you offer.

MARKETING STRATEGY: AN INVESTMENT OR EXPENSE? YOU DECIDE.

At the conclusion of each marketing strategy we will ask you whether you feel the idea is an investment or an expense.

Marketing is an investment to protect your investment. Your investment of course is your clients. In our opinion, the best pension plan that anyone can dream of. If you keep your clients happy, you will be able to work less and less, and make more and more money. Simply by keeping people happy. In addition, having a happy life-long relationship with your clients will increase the chance of your clients reaching their goals.

Marketing strategies vary in expense. We encourage you to consider the lifetime value of a client and what it means to you and your business, when you are considering the expense of a marketing strategy.

TAKE THE NEXT STEP WITH *THE PICTURE SELLS THE STORY™*

The financial world is complicated and overwhelming to most people, and I witnessed firsthand that clients won't buy what they don't understand. As an advisor, I recognized I was in the business of giving advice. It is up to the advisor to simplify concepts in order to better educate their clients. This idea ignited me to create easy to use illustrated financial concept explanations. I was able to take a complex idea, and have it be communicated and understood with a single image. Clients were able to absorb large amounts of data quickly to make the decisions process easier. From there *The Picture Sells the Story™* was born.

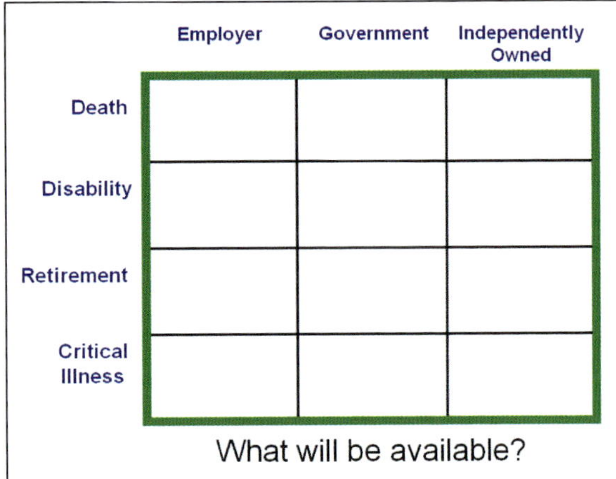

The original intent for my illustrated explanations was to be used as a tool during meetings to help my clients understand financial concepts. Today, successful financial advisors around the world are using them to move clients to action. If you purchased *The Loyalty Edge* alone, I encourage you to consider *The Picture Sells the Story™*.

For more information, please visit **www.ideasforadvisors.com**

When your clients feel confident in your guidance, they will be moved to action.

Client Name - Retired

No Boss
No Worries
No Meetings
No Responsibilities
Available 24/7 for Fun

ClientName@gmail.com
Cell: 222-333-4444
Follow my retirement on Facebook

Planned Ahead

Compliments of www.AdvisorName.com

CHAPTER 1

The Retirement Business Card

A Unique Tool to Keep Your Name Top of Mind with Clients and Prospects

Retirement brings many significant changes. Recognizing this momentous occasion is not only thoughtful, it is an important client appreciation strategy. One small change retirees have to accept is no longer having a business card. The majority of people spend their working years using business cards as a way to share their contact information. Here lies the void and the opportunity to give your clients a very unique retirement gift.

This client appreciation strategy recognizes a momentous occasion in a truly unique and special way.

A Retirement Business Card gives the client's contact information and a brief (humorous) note about their schedule as a retiree. The cards will read "*compliments of your firm or your name*" in the lower right. The minute your client gives someone their business card, the first question will be, '*Where did you get this?*'

Before sending out this piece, you must first imagine yourself as the client. Ask yourself, "Would I find this interesting and worth my time?"

MAKE AN UNFORGETTABLE IMPRESSION WITH RETIREMENT BUSINESS CARDS

Client appreciation is essential to client retention in any business. When a client feels valued and appreciated, the result will be a loyal client and an advocate for your business. To gain this loyalty, there are certain criteria that should be considered before sending out any client appreciation piece:

Let's see how the idea of Retirement Business Cards measure up to our *marketing strategy criteria for success*:

✔ Are you a credible source?

- You are a valued professional that brings new and impactful strategies.

✔ Do the cards differentiate you from others?

- These one-of-a-kind cards will help you stand out and keep your name top-of-mind.

✔ Are you creating an impact?

- Your clients/prospects will be delighted with their new business cards emphasize their lifestyle and leave an unforgettable impression.

✔ Are you establishing a long shelf life?

- These cards will continue building awareness of your services time and time again when they're passed out. Expect requests for more!

CENTERS OF INFLUENCE (COI)

Do you have a center of influence who is retiring but still very active in the community? A COI's ability to send you prospects does not diminish because they are no longer in practice. A retired lawyer on the golf course can be a very effective lead generator for you.

RETIREMENT BUSINESS CARD TEMPLATES

Before developing Retirement Business Cards, we encourage you to first speak to your client's spouse to find out what style of card would be appreciated. Some clients enjoy focusing on their current activities such as "still golfing," while others prefer to acknowledge their anticipated hobbies in retirement, for example *spending more time with grandchildren*. It's very important to use good judgment when deciding on exact wording.

It's also better to use a real photo of your client for the background of the card. Try to find one of them doing what they really enjoy; fishing, boating, reading, etc. You can even try to turn it into a caricature with photo retouching software.

Illustrated on the following pages are four Retirement Business Card templates, as well as accompanying memos to make implementing this in your own practice as easy as possible.

Template #1 — The Basic Retirement Business Card
Picture suggestions: fishing, gardening, hunting, boating, tennis

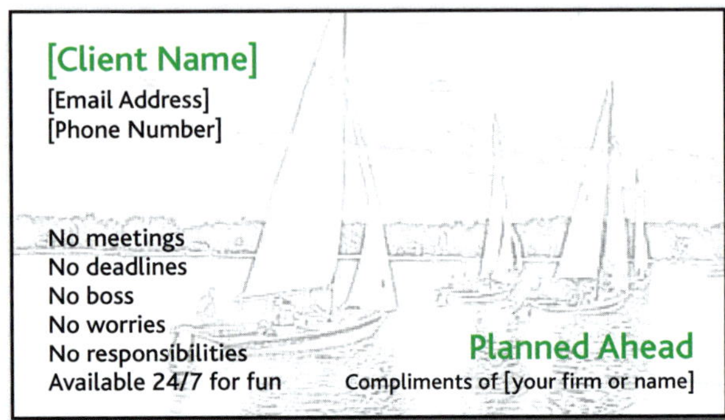

MEMO

Dear *Traditional Retirement Card,*

Congratulations on your retirement! This new journey will offer you many exciting opportunities, which I know you will embrace wholeheartedly!

Throughout your career, you have been used to carrying around business cards, so we thought you could use a retirement card that highlights your new activities.

In addition to your retirement, I would like to get together to talk about **government benefits (Canada Pension, Social Security)** and ensure you are maximizing what is available to you.

Please feel free to reach me at (your phone number) to set up a time and discuss your financial future in this new chapter in your life.

Sincerely,
Your Name

Template #2 — Soon to Be Retired
Picture suggestions: golfing, fishing, gardening

MEMO

Dear *Soon to be Retiree,*

You are close to embarking on a new journey in your life, filled with exciting opportunities and moments. Don't miss out on the top 5 activities in retirement:

- Travel
- Exercise
- Hobbies
- Family
- Leisure Activities

The truth is, these activities can be costly. I would like to get together with you to discuss how we can ensure that your retirement dreams become a reality.

Please feel free to reach me at (your phone number) to set up a time and discuss your financial future for the next chapter in your life.

Sincerely,
Your Name

P.S. I have sent along a box of retirement business cards that highlight your new role as a retiree.

Template #3 — Late Retiree
Picture suggestions: golfing, driving, yoga

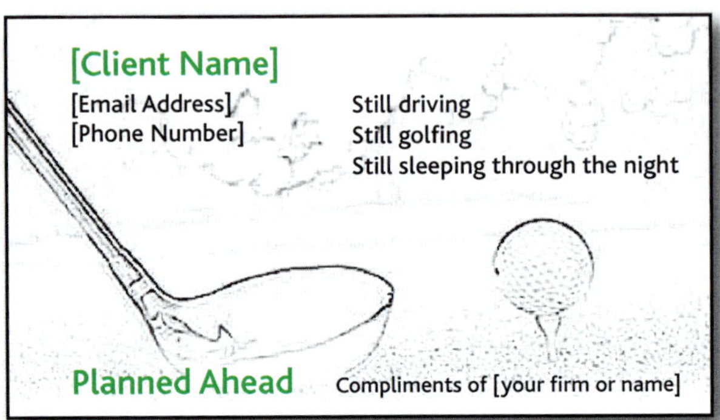

MEMO

Dear *Late Retiree,*

Top 5 activities in retirement:

- Travel
- Exercise
- Hobbies
- Family
- Leisure Activities

Each one of these can be costly, but I want to ensure you continue having a retirement filled with enjoyment. Let's sit down and talk about a **guaranteed 'play-check'** to cover your desired retirement activities.

Please feel free to reach me at (your phone number) to set up a time and discuss how you can enjoy an active retirement.

Sincerely,
Your Name

P.S. I have included a box of retirement business cards. I hope you have fun handing them out to your friends and family!

Template #4 – The Simple Business Card

Suitable for everyone, the retiree or not yet retired.

This could be used for a husband and wife.

Picture suggestions: Client's family

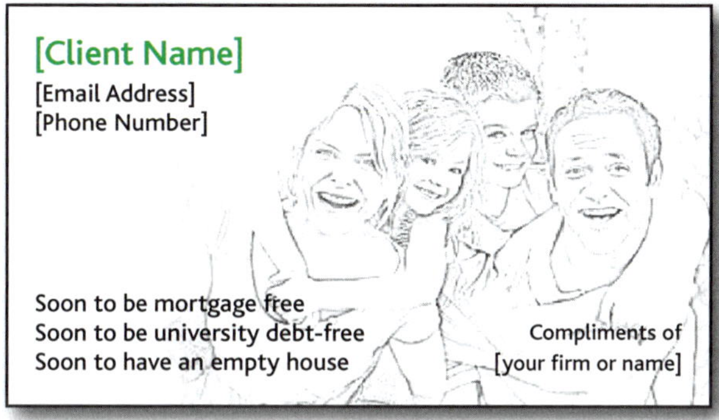

MEMO

Dear *Client – Simple Business Card*,

As a token to show our appreciation for putting your confidence and trust in our firm, we sent along a box of family contact cards. These are great to share with family and friends.

Thank you again for your continued work with (*your firm*)!

Sincerely,
Your Name

For templates, email michelle@ideasforadvisors.com

GENERATE GREAT RESULTS AND RESPONSES

Retirement Business Cards have been met with great response every time I share them. The time and effort you spend creating them for your clients will help you:

1. Generate quality referrals
2. Improve your client retention
3. Demonstrate your value proposition
4. Attract additional assets/insurance sales

Over the course of my career, many of my clients and centers of influence have received *Retirement Business Cards* as gifts from our office.

"I use them as contact information in my son's backpack. Such a useful gift."

"I am proud to hand them out – they capture all the things I love to do."

"I can't wait to hand these out on the golf course."

"This is the most unique gift I have ever received."

Ask Yourself...

Is the Retirement Business Card an investment or an expense?

It is an investment because it will
generate quality referrals and
demonstrate value with my client.

What if I had 5 clients each handing out 5 cards in the workplace, neighbourhood, to family, friends and at activities?

____

____

____

Which clients or centers of influence could I give retirement business cards to?

1. ______________________________
2. ______________________________
3. ______________________________

Which prospects?

1. ______________________________
2. ______________________________
3. ______________________________

Tasks that are easy to do are also easy not to do.

Dear Valued Client,

During the holiday season we are sponsoring your local neighbourhood watch program.

Wishing you and your family a safe holiday season.

Sincerely,
Your firm

CHAPTER 2

The Handwritten Card

When is the last time you received a handwritten card of appreciation?

If you are able to remember the last time you received a handwritten card of appreciation it is because of the impact it had on you, the way it made you feel. Today, we receive E-invitations, thank-you notes through Facebook messages, company updates on Twitter, and meeting confirmations via text. The handwritten card has become a thing of the past, yet it is one of the most valuable tools that can make a lasting impression.

For example, Doug Conant, the outgoing CEO of Campbell Soup and coauthor of *"Touchpoints,"* is a rare example of a CEO who truly appreciates the relationship between personal value and the bottom line. Over the past decade, Conant has spent at least an hour each day writing between 10 to 20 handwritten notes to colleagues in his company — welcoming new hires, thanking employees for their contributions, and congratulating leaders for specific accomplishments. This inspiring example carries a big commitment but results in loyal and motivated people who feel valued.

We recommend spending 30 minutes each week developing handwritten cards to send to your clients, centers of influence, friends or family members. Sending a handwritten note is an opportunity to nurture your relationships and show your appreciation. We have found it to be a timeless gift and the most powerful business tool for financial advisors.

The question I get asked the most is:

> "Mike, what one strategy do you suggest that I can add to my current systems that will have an immediate, positive impact on my business?

My answer:

> "Close your door for 30 minutes each week, and send out four high quality, handwritten cards or notes of appreciation."

CELEBRATE THE HOLIDAYS WITH CARDS

You can choose the traditional path of sending cards for common holidays (Christmas, Easter etc.) or you can set yourself apart with cards for unique holidays. (The following is a list for your reference or you can google: unique or special holidays for more choices.) For example, if you have clients who are doctors, reward them with a card on National Doctors' Day, or send a card to all your clients who are teachers on National Teachers' Day. Be inspired to recognize unique days and holidays, as this creates a *wow-gesture*. These timely yet unexpected cards will keep you top-of-mind with your clients.

Remember to listen! Take notes on important events and birthdays for a client's child and spouse, such as a birthday, graduation, wedding, etc.

Unique Holidays to Consider:

New Years	January 1st
Employee Appreciation Day	First Friday in March
National Mom and Pop Business Owners Day	March 29th
National Doctors' Day	March 30th
Easter	varies: late March or April
Administrative Professionals' Day	Wednesday of last full week in April
National Nurses' Day	May 6th
National Receptionist Day	Second Wednesday in May
Mother's Day	Second Sunday in May
Father's Day	Third Sunday in June
Canada Day	July 1st
Independence Day	July 4th
National Thank You Day	September 15th
Grandparents Day	First Sunday after Labor Day
World Teachers' Day	October 5th
Boss's Day	October 16th
Thanksgiving	Last Thursday in November
Christmas	December 25th
Centers of Influence Day	Pick any date you want to acknowledge this special relationship

Google "Special Holidays" to find interesting days to acknowledge with your clients.

WHAT SHOULD I SAY?

The first step is to have plenty of high quality cards in your office. These should include not only thank you cards but also sympathy, congratulations and blank cards. Having an inventory of cards in your office will help you avoid procrastination — tasks that are easy to do are also easy not to do.

One of the reasons people don't send out cards is that they don't know what to say. Below are four templates to make the process **easier for you**. These can be used exactly as they appear, or you can tweak them to fit your situation.

Example 1 — After a meeting with an existing client

Dear Client,

I am sending you a brief note to let you know how much I have enjoyed our meetings over the past years.

I appreciate the confidence you have placed in me, and I look forward to our continued work together.

Please feel free to call me anytime.

All my best.

Sincerely,
Your Name

Example 2 — For a new client after an initial meeting

Dear Client,

I look forward to the opportunity of working with you and appreciate the confidence you have placed in me.

Please feel free to call me anytime.

All the best.

Sincerely,
Your Name

Example 3 — To thank a client for a referral

Dear Client,

Thanks again for the referral to (referral's name).

I want to assure you that whether or not they become a client, I appreciate this introduction.

You can rest assured that I will treat your (friend/family) with professionalism and respect.

All my best.

Regards,
Your Name

If you decide you want to send a handwritten card after every client appointment, be sure to make it part of your post-meeting task list.

Example 4 — For a prospect after an initial meeting

> *Dear Client,*
>
> *It was a pleasure meeting with you last week.*
>
> *I am certain that we can help your financial needs.*
>
> *As discussed, I will follow up with you next month. However, if you would like to discuss anything, please feel free to contact us.*
>
> *All my best.*
>
> *Sincerely,*
> *Your Name*

MAKE AN UNFORGETTABLE IMPRESSION WITH HANDWRITTEN CARDS

Let's see how the idea of handwritten cards measure up to our marketing strategy criteria for success:

✔ Are you a credible source?

- You will be seen as authentic and thoughtful because you are setting yourself a part.

✔ Do the cards differentiate you from others?

- In today's digital society, you will stand out with this timeless gesture of appreciation.

✔ Are you creating an impact?

- You are making a huge impact by taking the time to write a thoughtful note, which will be positively recognized.

✔ Are you establishing a long shelf life?

- Your clients/prospects will appreciate your gesture and it will work towards building long-lasting relationships.

Ask Yourself...

Is the Handwritten Card an investment or an expense?

It is an investment because it will generate quality referrals and demonstrate value with my client.

Which clients, centers of influence or prospects could I send handwritten cards to?

1. ______________________________

2. ______________________________

3. ______________________________

How would my business look in 12 months if I take 15 minutes each week to send handwritten notes of appreciation?

____

____

____

A real idea that real advisors have used on real clients to generate big results.

Go Back on the Dole

Neither Tories Nor Laborites Will Consent To Coalition Government

STATE THE TOPEKA JOURNAL

NIKI RENEWS 'TALK' PLE

Bob Sounds Berlin Warnin

The New York Times.

LATE CITY EDITION

NTER ORBITS EARTH 3 TIMES SAFELY, OVERSHOOTS LANDING AREA 250 MILES; E IN DOUBT AN HOUR, HE IS FOUND IN

THIS WORLD TODAY

San Francisco Chronicle

CHURCHILL BLAMES L REGIME FOR COAL CR

Britain by Candlelight

Churchill Blames Laborites for Coal Crisis

School Bus Ruling

The Evening Star

Metropolitan Edition

Iceman Lands After 25 He

Dillon to Outline Goal For Social Revolution

Starts Today–Yogi Bear Color Comic–See Part 7

Chicago Sunday Tribune

CITY FINAL

PUT 7 TON SPUTNIK IN ORBIT

REDS GIVE NO HINT OF ANY LIFE ABOARD

17 Inch Snow Cripples N. Y. City

Navy Orders Speedup of 5 Polaris Subs

Satellite Biggest in Space Race

STORM HALTS AIR AND SHIP MOVEMENTS

Batters Much of New England

Happy Reunion Day

Dela orecast f Highways, New B

CHAPTER 3

Historic Newspaper

Striving to be successful?
The #1 ingredient: excitement!

At Ideas for Advisors, we strive to provide effective and exciting ideas to inspire you to take your business to the next level. Our goal is to ignite your creative energy with easy to implement ideas that will make a difference in your business today, and help you better engage your clients to make a lasting impression.

One of the best ways to capture and keep a client's attention is to simply ask yourself, "How will this make my client feel?" In my own early stage of prospecting, I asked myself this simple question, and I found great success. It made me want to find ways to ensure my clients felt valued, and were excited in the planning process. You may be thinking, 'Is it even possible for a financial advisor to have clients who are excited to do business with them?'

The answer is absolutely, as long as you're passionate and eager to work with them. However, the key is to make sure your spirit of enthusiasm is transferred to your client. It is a human core emotional need to feel val-

Historic newspapers are easy to order. Find companies on page 38.

ued. Whether or not a person feels acknowledged and appreciated influences their behavior, consumes their energy and affects their decisions all day long, whether they're aware of it or not.

If you maintain an ongoing client recognition program, you will boost client engagement, foster loyalty, and retain existing clients while attracting new prospects. This will have a direct and positive impact on your bottom line. There are many ways to stay and get in front of high-quality clients/prospects, but one of the most effective ways to stay top-of-mind is by giving a gift that gets them to say, "Wow!"

NOSTALGIC GIFT FROM THE PAST

A real idea that creates impactful results is the historical newspaper from the day your client/prospect was born. The real, authentic historic newspaper is a unique way to commemorate a birthday, anniversary, retirement, etc. It is an original newspaper from a person's special day that comes with a collector's certificate of authenticity. You can send a newspaper from *The New York Times, LA Times, Boston Globe,* etc. This gives prospects and clients the rare opportunity to look back in time. By giving this exciting gift, you are instilling excitement within your client that will resonate back to you. We have given the historic newspaper to countless clients, and have seen real results.

A friend of mine and a fellow Million Dollar Round Table (MDRT), The Premier Association of Financial Professionals, member shared his story about how he used the historic newspaper marketing strategy. This is his story:

> "I had a very good client who was celebrating his 50th birthday and his employees were having a party for him. I wanted to do something to commemorate his special day, so I decided on the historic newspaper. I knew it was a great idea but I did not expect the response from everyone at the party, including my client. They really were in awe of the newspaper which started new conversations with potential clients."

He opened great, new accounts with targeted clients but more importantly, he connected with everyone at the party on a very personal level that day. The advisor demonstrated extreme forethought, and was seen by everyone as thoughtful and competent. The client also felt valued, appreciated and special. In return, the client shared their newspaper with others, which created targeted referrals for my fellow MDRT member.

The historical newspaper is one of our most favorite ways to show our clients and centers of influence that we value them, as well as a great way to get our name in front of prospects. When people receive this gift, they too will want to show their friends, just like the Retirement Business Card (see Chapter 1). Their friends will automatically ask where they got it, and your name will arise.

People don't care how much you know, until they know how much you care. The historical newspaper shows current clients that you planned a thoughtful gift, and it also shows prospects that you are going the extra mile to get to know them. This gift helps create the feeling of appreciation.

Let's see how this idea measures up to our *Marketing Strategy Criteria for Success:*

✔ Are you a credible source?

- You will set yourself apart as someone who is thoughtful, thus lending you as their primary advisor.

✔ Differentiate you from others?

- This gift is a great way to nurture and kick-start a meaningful connection with your clients/prospects.

✔ High impact?

- It helps you build and cement your business relationships, because you sent a personalized and unique gift.

✔ A long shelf life?

- The historic newspaper is a great conversation starter. Often times, it becomes a coffee table book at home, or displayed on a person's desk at work. Your client/prospect will be eager to share interesting sections of the newspaper with everyone they know, and your name will continue being shared.

We have discovered that many countries offer historic newspapers in their National Library and are available for sale on microfilms. To name a few are Singapore, Southeast Asia, Ireland, Australia and Finland. You can check out which country has them available by searching the National Library newspaper microfilm on Google.

Here are a couple of choices for purchasing historical newspapers:

- **www.simplypersonalized.com**
- **www.anydate.com**
- **www.birthdayandanniversarygifts.com**

If you have already given an historical newspaper as a gift, try one of these great alternatives:

- A historical magazine; **www.oldmags.com**
- A personalized birthday letter with facts from their date of the birth; **www.thepeoplehistory.com**
- Retro music cd from their year of birth; **www.simplypersonalized.com**

THE LETTER

Below you will find two sample letters to accompany the historic newspaper (or one of the alternative unique gifts from the past). The first one is an example of a letter you can send to a prospect, and the second one is what you can send to a client. Yours may vary depending on if you are sending the newspaper for a birthday, retirement, anniversary, etc. You also need to take into consideration the interests of the person you are sending the newspaper to; this will help you decide which topics of interest to highlight.

From our experience writing letters, we recommend:

- Keeping it short; less than eight sentences.
- Use Wikipedia or The Peoples History to call out interesting facts about what happened in that year.
- Keeping it conversational, but sincere.
- Writing the letter on vintage-style paper to really give the gift a classic feel.

Example One: Prospect

Dear Prospect,

I have been hoping our paths would cross and we would have the good fortune of meeting one another. Since that time hasn't come yet, I'd like to introduce myself to you.

My name is Advisor Name, and I am a financial advisor who has been in practice for ( ) years. One of the most fulfilling aspects of my job is educating people to make informed decisions about their financial futures. There are many pieces to the financial puzzle, and I truly enjoy helping people put those pieces together.

I will follow up with you in a few of days to see if you have any interest in learning more about how we can help you towards a secure financial plan.

P.S. Enclosed is a real, authentic newspaper from the day you were born. Interesting to note (include an interesting reference from the newspaper). It is truly amazing to see how things have changed, and I hope you enjoy delving into the archive of times gone by.

Sincerely,
Your Name

Example Two: Client

Dear Client,

Congratulations on your 65th Birthday!

I thought you might find this original Boston Globe from the day you were born to be an interesting look back in time. I hope you enjoy delving into the archive of times gone by.

It's amazing to see how things have changed, such as (include five interesting bullet points, referencing from the newspaper):

- The big stars of the silver screen of 1942 were James Cagney in *Yankee Doodle Dandy* and Clark Gable and Lana Turner in *Some Where I'll Find You.*
- The United States Postal Service was in the process of releasing a new 3-cent stamp.
- Classified ads were broken down into help wanted male and female sections.
- Anne Frank started writing her diary.

Thank you for your ongoing support, I appreciate having you as a client and happy birthday!

Sincerely,
Your Name

TREAT YOURSELF

Don't forget to order your own historic newspaper from the day you were born for the perfect meeting-room marketing piece. It serves as a great conversation piece, but more importantly it is a powerful tool to illustrate what the market has done over your lifetime. Your presentations will be much more compelling when you use this unique piece as an example of growth.

Ask Yourself…

Is the Historic Newspaper an investment or an expense?

It is an investment because it is
so unique and has incredible impact.

What would be the return on investment if I had 5 clients or centers of influence displaying and sharing this gift from me with others?

Which clients or centers of influence could I send an historic newspaper to?

1. __________
2. __________
3. __________

Which prospects?

1. __________
2. __________
3. __________

Show your clients that you value their confidence and trust in you.

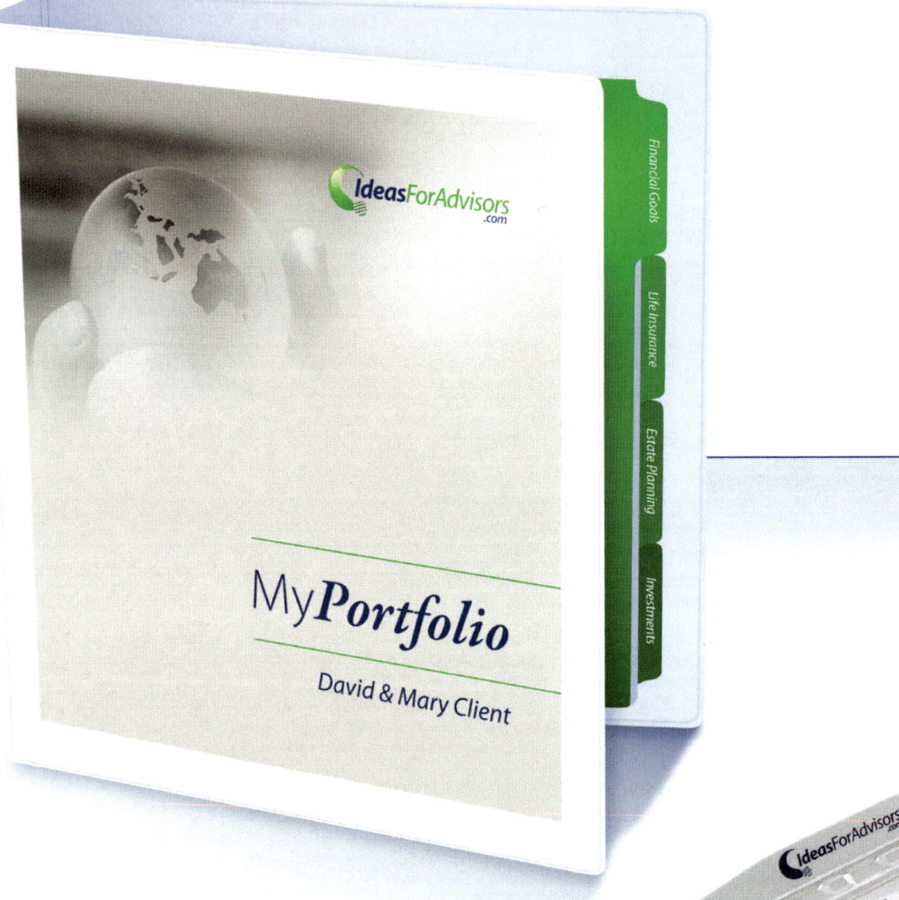
IdeasForAdvisors.com
Financial Goals
Life Insurance
Estate Planning
Investments
MyPortfolio
David & Mary Client

CHAPTER 4

The Financial Organizer

Your clients will say:
"Thanks for getting us organized."

Ensuring you have strategies in place that foster loyalty and provide value are an integral part of business operations. Client appreciation gifts are just one way to demonstrate you value your clients' trust and confidence. In addition to the gifts we mentioned in the previous chapters, we have found the gift of a financial organizer to be an ideal way to show clients your dedication in helping them develop a sound financial plan.

Every sound financial plan includes document record keeping and organization. A financial organizer enables quick and easy retrieval of statements from other institutions, mortgage statements, tax information and much more. It becomes a valuable strategy for gathering all of a client's financial information, and gives you an opportunity to uncover additional opportunities.

This is also a great way to get your clients hands-on in the planning process, because they will be able to see all the parts that make up their financial plan in one easy to digest binder. This gift will help them visualize all the components they need to share with you in order for you to provide the best advice possible. In return, client meetings will be much more productive and effective.

HOW TO CREATE A FINANCIAL ORGANIZER BINDER

We have found that a 3 inch binder with a plastic framed view cover to be the most successful. The plastic cover allows you to insert a 8.5" x 11" custom printed cover and back. On the cover, you can include your firm's name, logo and contact information, as well as the client's name. On the back cover, you can add your firm's promise or elevator speech. Even the spine of the binder allows you to promote your brand and professional image, so make sure you think strategically. Inside the binder, include customized labeled tabs. For example, they can say: Financial Goals, Life Insurance, Investments, Mortgage, Wills, Estate Planning, Statements, Employee Benefits, and General Information.

Make sure when you call your clients about their upcoming appointments, you remind them to bring their financial organizer.

Even if your client doesn't use their financial organizer, your efforts will not be wasted because they'll appreciate the thought behind the gift. They will see that they are valued, which has potential to increase your referrals.

DON'T FORGET TO ADD THAT EXTRA TOUCH

Impress your clients even more by including a paper hole punch with their financial organizer binder; another thoughtful gesture to keep your clients organized. You can even customize the paper hole punch with your company logo. It's always a great idea to deliver packages personally, but we have found another method that has proven to have more impact – direct mail. You can purchase cardboard boxes in bulk, so they are always on-hand, and send the contents of the binder and the paper hole punch in a box through the mail. Your client will receive a pick-up slip from the Post Office, which lends to a degree of anticipation, surprise and then appreciation.

Let's see how this idea measures up to our *Marketing Strategy Criteria for Success*:

✔ Are you a credible source?

- The financial organizer demonstrates that you take your client's financial future seriously with the special attention you are giving their financial needs.

✔ Differentiate you from others?

- Putting together a unique and customized financial organizer shows that you put forth effort and extra attention to clients' needs.

✔ High impact?

- Your thoughtfulness will be valued because you put your clients' best interest first, and great referrals will be inevitable.

✔ A long shelf life?

- The financial organizer is a simple way to help clients feel in control and organized in meetings, which will be used every time you two meet or when they need to go over their paperwork with loved ones.

Ask Yourself...

Is the Financial Organizer an investment or an expense?

It is an investment because my clients will truly appreciate my efforts.

Which 5 clients could I give the financial organizer to?

1. __________
2. __________
3. __________
4. __________
5. __________

Which centers of influence or prospects could I give the financial organizer to?

1. __________
2. __________
3. __________
4. __________
5. __________

What are you going to do this year to attract and retain more clients?

CHAPTER 5

Grow Your Business by Generating Targeted, High Quality Referrals

Your clients want the opportunity to help those they care about.

Whether you are a new or seasoned advisor, we all know how important a steady stream of referrals are to the success of our business. Having a positive endorsement from a client can have a huge impact on your prospect pipeline. So why is it that we covet for referrals, yet don't pursue them as much as we should?

We're going to take a closer look at your current referral system and explore new effective strategies that you can implement today to generate even more results. From creating word-of-mouth buzz to delivering a knock-out letter of introduction, *Ideas for Advisors* will provide you the resources you need to optimize your business and relationships.

Studies have found that a majority of engaged clients who refer had been asked for feedback, and 72% believe that the feedback they provided made a real difference.

ARE YOU AND YOUR FIRM REFERABLE?

The way to attract referrals is to have a "build it and they will come" philosophy. Most advisors have built their foundation by developing good habits such as delivering what is promised, being punctual to meetings and always acting with professionalism and integrity. Now, what else are you and *your firm* doing? When a client comes in for a meeting they remember not only you, but the environment you provide. To make you and your firm more referable, try incorporating these techniques:

- Provide refreshments and snacks in your lobby
- Have publications that you've been quoted in or featured displayed on a table
- Have a parking spot saved for the client/prospect that is coming in and put their name on it

ARE YOU VOCAL ABOUT REFERRALS?

One of the biggest challenges an advisor faces regarding referrals, is simply not asking for them. Your clients need to know you are open for business, so it is your job to communicate your specialty. A few simple words on your business cards, email signature, website and newsletters will help to convey that you are accepting new clients. Below are some examples of what you can add to your marketing materials:

- Referrals appreciated
- By referral only
- Referral-based
- Client-centered
- The greatest compliment we receive is a referral from you
- A referral from a satisfied client is a huge responsibility and something we never take lightly
- We earn our client's trust and respect by protecting them on the downside

ARE YOU COMMUNICATING YOUR EXPERTISE?

The clearer you are about what you offer and who can benefit from your help, the easier it will be for your client to tell their friend, family member, etc. Your clients can't share what your specialty is, unless you communicate it to them regularly. Your clients should know the answers to the below questions to make an easy segue to referrals that fit your market:

- What makes you different?
- What is your unique value?
- Who is your target market?
- What areas of finance do you specialize in?

ARE YOU REACHABLE?

The final question you need to ask yourself is, "Am I making it easy for clients to give me a referral?" Use client meetings as an opportunity to collect referrals and to show a sample letter of introduction that you would send the prospect - and the process you would go through. Your client needs to be reassured that you are going to treat the referral with true professionalism.

You can open your discussion by saying, "One of our goals for this year is to add several new clients to our firm. Do you know of someone that values helpful advice? I want to assure you that we will handle any referral that you give us with the utmost professionalism. For example, I want to share with you the letter of introduction that I would send to someone that you refer to me."

THE LETTER OF INTRODUCTION

A letter of introduction is a note that is used to write someone introducing yourself and the services you provide, in hopes of securing a meeting to further discuss how you can work together.

There is no one size fits all for a letter of introduction. You need to tweak each letter you write to fit the needs and interests of the person you are contacting. Following are five simple tips to help you develop a professional and effective letter of introduction.

Tip 1: Introduction vs. referral

We suggest that when communicating with a client or prospect, you should use the word *introduced* or *introduction*.

Tip 2: Focus on a referral's needs

Make sure to emphasize why the prospect should see you in the first few lines of the letter. People like to know what's in it for them and how they will benefit. You need a clear and compelling answer to, "Why should they give up their time to see me?"

Tip 3: Capture a referral's attention

Include something of interest when sending your letter of introduction. This may be an article, brochure or book that aligns with their hobby, financial scenario or something your client who referred them shared. The key is in knowing what would appeal to the referral. Ask the right questions of the client so that you have a good understanding of them.

Tip 4: Get clients involved

Sometimes clients are reluctant on giving referrals, so eliminate the hesitation by involving them in the process. Ask for their feedback on you, as an advisor, your firm, your services, etc. Find out what services they value, what they would like to see changed or added. You can do this during meetings, client surveys and client advisory boards, which are the most effective means of client involvement. The client survey will provide a broad collection from a large group of clients; the advisory board will provide more concise information from a select group of clients. A more engaged client will be more open to giving you introductions.

Tip 5: Include a carbon copy

The most important part of the letter of introduction is the carbon copy that gets sent to the client. The referral will see a copy of the letter going to your client, who may be their friend, coworker, family member, etc., which increases your chances of securing a meeting. The referral may contact your client to get more information about you. The conversation that comes up as a result of the carbon copy will be in your favor because your client trusts and believes that their friends/family should be working with you since they gave you the referral.

Example of a letter of introduction

Dear *(Referral)*,

A mutual friend, *(Client)*, suggested that I touch base and introduce myself. My name is *(Your name)*, and I am financial advisor with *(Your firm)*.

We believe everyone's situation is unique and as such requires a personalized approach. In my experience, minor adjustments lead to major improvements. *(Client)* mentioned you might find value in the personalized service we offer regarding financial needs, especially post-secondary financial plans.

With teenage children, I imagine the idea of college is becoming a close reality. I've enclosed some information that highlights all the resources available to parents of college students. I would be happy to discuss this more in detail with you, and come up with a unique financial plan that fits your needs.

You can trust that our meeting together will be a good investment of your time. I sincerely hope that this information is of value to you. I will contact you in the near future to discuss how our education planning may benefit you.

Sincerely,
(Your Name)

cc: *(Client)*

YOU'RE NOT DONE YET

It's important not to forget to say thank you to your client for the referral, whether or not you get an appointment. You need to show your gratitude and appreciation if you want that client to give you a referral again. In addition to sending your client a thank you note, you should reach out to the referral as well to thank them for their consideration. Below are a few variations of notes you can send:

Example 1 — Thank you to the client

Dear (Client),

Thank you for introducing me to (Referral). I want to assure you that whether or not they become a client, they will be treated with respect and professionalism. I appreciate your confidence in the services we offer.

Sincerely,
(Your Name)

Example 2 — Thank you to the referral; intent on doing business

Dear (Referral),

I look forward to the opportunity of working with you and appreciate the confidence you have placed in me. Please feel free to call me anytime.

Sincerely,
(Your Name)

Example 3 — Thank you to the referral; no intent on doing business at the moment

Dear (Referral),

It was a pleasure speaking with you. If your needs change or if you decide you would like a second opinion on your current financial plan, please don't hesitate to contact me.

Sincerely,
(Your Name)

Let's see how this idea measures up to our *Marketing Strategy Criteria for Success*:

✔ Does the information establish you as a credible source?

- The letter of introduction will establish you as a credible source in the eyes of the prospect, because they will see their family member, friend, etc. referred you to them, which is a testament that you manage finances, with professionalism and integrity.

✔ Is it going to differentiate you from everyone else?

- By including your clients in the development of the letter of introduction, it will greatly set you apart because they will remember how you asked for their advice and opinions.

✔ Does it have high impact?

- Sending out a letter of introduction creates great impact because you get affirmation you're exceeding your client's expectations with the referral they gave you.

✔ Does it have a long shelf life?

- The letter of introduction leads it way to a fruitful, potential relationship with a prospect that can continue to grow over the years.

Ask Yourself...

Should I have a referral system?

Yes, I should! It is the #1 way to grow my business.

What would my business look like if I had only 5 introductions each month?

Which referral strategies am I going to implement immediately?

Transform knowing into doing.

CHAPTER 6

The Elevator Speech

Who Are You and What Do You Do?

If you were in front of a dream prospect, could you deliver your value proposition in a way that is so compelling that it moves them to action? 7 Seconds to make a powerful, lasting impression and prospects who say, Tell Me More!

Personal encounters happen every single day, whether you are having a business meeting, out networking with other professionals or just mingling with friends. Two common questions that typically come up during these occasions are "What do you do for a living?" Or, "Can you tell me more about yourself?" When asked one of these questions directly, you need to be ready with an 'elevator speech.'

The term elevator speech comes from the notion that you should be able to explain to someone who you are, what you do and what you're interested in, in the amount of time it takes to ride an elevator. An elevator speech is as essential as a business card and should make people want to learn more about you and your company.

For example, if you were in front of a dream prospect, could you deliver your value proposition in a way that is so compelling that it moves them to action? A prospect will decide within the first few seconds whether or not they want to hear more. In today's world, people have become instant decision makers. We receive thousands of commercial messages/day. Each message lasting between 5 and 15 seconds. A prospect will decide within the first 7 seconds whether or not they want to hear more.

The way we socialize and meet prospects has changed. Today it is a social platform not an elevator platform. We strive to engage not convince. But the premise is the same — the ability to deliver your value proposition in a way that would make them say, "Tell Me More!"

To help you engage prospects and leave a lasting, powerful impression, use these three suggestions to prepare and deliver a memorable elevator speech.

1. Know your audience

Before figuring out what you're going to say in your elevator speech, you need to figure out who your audience is. It's important to tailor your speech to the individual you're speaking to, because one 'generic' speech is certain to fail. When you have a clear vision of your audience, you can customize your speech and focus your message on their needs.

2. Know yourself

Once you know your target audience, you need to figure out what makes you unique and why they should listen to you. To help you hone in on your skills, ask yourself these three questions:

1. What makes me unique?
2. What problems can I solve?
3. What benefits do I provide?

If you focus on these questions, it will be easier to drill down what makes you and your company stand out. Write down a few different statements and test them out to see what gets the best response, but make sure your explanations are defined, compelling and memorable. The ultimate goal is clarity. Everything a company embarks on should emanate from that core purpose.

3. Be natural

Once you have you outlined your responses, you need to get comfortable. Practice saying it out loud as much as you can. Writing is more formal and structured than speaking, so you may need to tweak your words. You want it to feel natural and spark interest with your listener; you don't want to sound like a pre-recorded program. Once you feel confident in your speech, practice on a friend and ask them what they thought your key points were.

As you get used to delivering your pitch, you'll notice engagement with listeners will increase and you'll start hearing, "Tell me more."

Powerful words and phrasing are essential to grab the listener's attention and make an impact. Here are some words that will add flare to your pitch: established, foremost, key, leading, main, original, pioneering, predominant, preferred, premier, progressive, recognized, accomplished, achieve, benefit, compelling, convenient, exciting, improve, proven, quality, safe, solution, strong, top, uncover, unique, winning, amazing.

Some examples that we feel hit the mark!

"I'm mortar. I make sure a family's wealth does not crumble between generations."

"Have you ever looked at the directions to put together an IKEA piece of furniture? I put together people's 'financial furniture.' I take the gibberish and complication out of people's financial situations and put them together quickly and efficiently so they can enjoy them."

"We provide solutions to help people sleep better at night."

"Our role is to help our clients make smart financial decisions regarding their personal and business financial planning."

"I sell umbrellas when it is sunny."

"We answer the question that everyone wants an answer to: Will I have enough money to last me for the rest of my life, in the manner to which I have become accustomed?"

"My team develops financial plans that ensure that they have the means to realize their dreams. Our success is seeing our clients succeed."

Use your elevator speech everywhere. On your letterhead, in your marketing materials, as a tagline on your emails — everywhere!

Ask Yourself...

What makes me unique?

What problems can I solve?

What benefits do I provide?

Put it all together.

My elevator speech is...

There is a direct and critical link between a client who feels valued and their loyalty to you.

CHAPTER 7

Impressive Policy Delivery

As an industry, we tend to dismiss the importance of the simple, time-honoured, personal gestures. This reigns true when selling a life insurance policy. Many advisors think when they make a sale, their work is done. However, did you know selling a life insurance policy has one final step?

To maintain a superior level of client service, advisors must be invested in providing high-impact marketing strategies to satisfy a client's needs and expectations. One way to add value and enhance your credibility is through the policy delivery. The policy delivery is an opportunity to set you apart as a professional who is invested in their clients and goes the extra mile. To improve your service standards, consider the following suggestions:

Personally deliver the policy: Make the intangible, tangible by delivering the policy in-person. It's a unique way to leave a positive and lasting impression. It will elevate the entire sales experience and assure your client that they made an important decision in protecting what matters most to them.

Deliver a custom package: When a client receives their policy in a high-quality wallet or customized handcrafted case, the importance of their decision is emphasized. You can also give your client their policy in their very own custom folder, which they can use to keep other pertinent documents in. When used, they'll remember your delivery.

Give supporting information: Make sure to include any extra documents that provide guidance about their policy or to help with their financial future. For example, you can include *I am Your Life Insurance Policy Letter, Your Will Planning Workbook, The Financial Priority Pyramid,* and *Get Organized/ Budget Worksheet.* You can find these in the supporting documents section of this chapter. Or, if you would like a hard copy of any of these, please contact us at michelle@ideasforadvisors.com.

Plant seeds for future discussions: When delivering the policy, use that time as an opportunity to layout your customer service standards. Discuss what they can expect from a communication perspective and how often you want to meet with them. It's important to strategize the next step in their financial security plan.

Referrals: Now that your current policy delivery system is referral worthy, be sure to let your clients know that you are open for business and that referrals are always appreciated. Or, you can include extra business cards in your policy delivery package.

Write a congratulatory letter: You can avoid buyer's remorse by sending a client a handwritten note congratulating them on taking a major step toward a secure financial future. The decision to purchase life insurance means spending money on something they will never see. This letter will help the client gain confidence that you have the expertise to guide them to a policy that ensures their future financial security.

CONGRATULATORY CLIENT NOTE

To grow your business, you need to look at the way you present yourself. There is a direct and critical link between a client who feels valued and their loyalty to you. Everyone appreciates the expression of gratitude, and this is particularly true in the insurance business.

Taking the time to thank a client is an excellent way to demonstrate the caring and attentive advisor you are. These letters will go a long way toward not only expressing your gratitude, but your professionalism and dedication as well. Everything you do either adds or subtracts to the value that you provide to clients and prospects.

Sample 1

Dear *Client*,

It was a pleasure meeting with you today. We appreciate the faith and confidence you have placed in us as your Financial Planner. We recognize that you have many choices and we thank you for choosing us.

We will work hard to deserve your confidence and we are ready to take your call if you have any questions.

Sincerely,
(Your Name)

Sample 2

Dear *Client*,

Thank you for meeting with me today. I appreciate your confidence in choosing us to manage your financial security needs.

We would like to take this time to congratulate you on taking this step toward your family's financial security.

The entire team at (*your firm*) is looking forward to working with you.

Sincerely,
(Your Name)

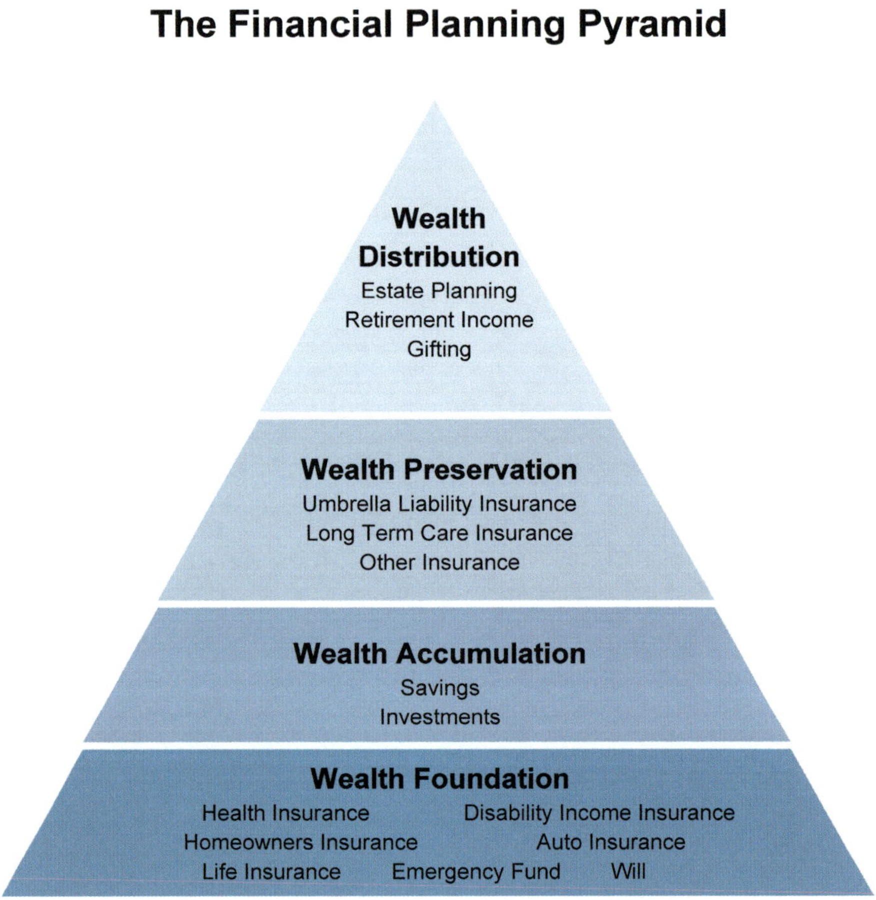

The Financial Planning Pyramid

Wealth Distribution
Estate Planning
Retirement Income
Gifting

Wealth Preservation
Umbrella Liability Insurance
Long Term Care Insurance
Other Insurance

Wealth Accumulation
Savings
Investments

Wealth Foundation
Health Insurance
Disability Income Insurance
Homeowners Insurance
Auto Insurance
Life Insurance
Emergency Fund
Will

For an editable version of the Financial Pyramid and other supporting documents, such as *The Will Planning Workbook* and a budget module, *Getting Organized*, please email: michelle@ideasforadvisors.com.

ARE YOU BUILDING CLIENT APPRECIATION?

I find myself in many different cities speaking at events worldwide. I enjoy having this time to talk to advisors, some who write million dollar cases, others who are just getting started in the business. What all advisors have in common is their drive to keep their clients happy. Knowing that it is much easier to keep a client than to find a new one, advisors hope that their systems are value-based and effective. By incorporating an impressive policy delivery process, you will be on your way to building long-term relationships.

Make yourself
better than you were
the day before.

CHAPTER 8

Small Incremental Steps

Success in any industry results from compound interest, such as specialized knowledge and strategic systems. Those that breed productivity put forth the effort to advance their education and develop a process that works best for them. Everyone has the opportunity to be successful. We just have to do the right things right and more importantly; we have to do them frequently. However, the problem is that most people get stuck between wanting to do something and actually doing it. We all want to make positive changes but sometimes the challenge seems insurmountable.

If you take small incremental steps every day, you can eliminate the gap. In looking at my own practice, the four elements outlined below have proved to be the most important in achieving prosperity, and they too can add a cutting-edge advantage to your practice:

CONTROL INTERRUPTIONS

We live in a world full of daily interruptions from instant messaging to texts, emails, phone calls and even people simply walking through the door. While these interruptions can lead to potential business, they still remove you from what you were working on. Take control of the distractions that are destroying your productivity by trying these useful tips:

- **Schedule a specific time to answer emails and text messages**. Don't let answering emails and texts consume your whole day. Set aside a specific period of time to respond to clients, but make sure you let them know you may not respond instantly. They will appreciate knowing when they will hear from you and your time management skills.

- **Get to the office an hour earlier**. Jump start your day by arriving to the office an hour earlier. This extra hour of free time can be used to organize, goal-set and plan out your day or weeks ahead. This will eliminate having to take time out of the middle of your busy workday, and instead give you the time to focus your efforts elsewhere.

- **Give yourself one hour away from the computer**. There is no denying that the rise of the computer coupled with the increasing availability of high-speed internet, has impacted our daily lives. Today we get caught up searching the Web, answering emails, tweeting, Facebooking, client work, blogging etc. We have turned one of our biggest advantages in the workplace into one of our biggest distractions. Cut down on your computer usage and tighten up on becoming more efficient with what you have sitting in front of you, by using an app called Freedom. It temporarily disables your network, and prevents you from visiting websites, sending or receiving email or anything else internet related for a self-selected amount of time.

BE AN EARLY RISER

The saying goes "the early bird catches the worm," so it shouldn't be a surprise that the early bird schedule is the routine for many successful professionals. Several studies have correlated waking up early with success because people are more likely to anticipate problems, prioritize tasks they want to accomplish, identify long-range goals and be more optimistic. Also, early in the morning is commonly the most quiet and uninterrupted time of the day, which allows one to completely focus on what's at-hand. For those less inclined to become early risers, it is possible with a little willpower strengthening. Willpower is a muscle that can be exercised and made stronger every day. Try the following tips to become an early riser:

- **Choose to get up before you go to sleep**. Make your decision to rise at a specific time before you go to sleep the night before. Follow your decision and hold yourself accountable to this decision like you do with anything else in your life.
- **Exercise**. Make working out part of your early morning routine. Regular exercise boosts mood and provides energy on the job, it also helps create deeper sleep cycles.
- **Reward yourself**. Right when you wake up do something that you enjoy such as drinking a nice cup of coffee or tea, sitting and reading the newspaper or mediating. Find something that's pleasurable for you, and allow yourself to do it as part of your morning routine.

Small changes equal small victories that lead to the life you want. We all want to make positive changes but sometimes the challenge seems insurmountable.

EMBRACE TECHNOLOGY

Technology can be a friend and an enemy. If you can keep it from being a distraction and use it to your advantage, it really makes life easier, more effective and successful. Take control of technology and reap in its benefits by:

- **Develop a website**. The number one rule is to make sure you keep your site simple, so readers can easily navigate through the information. Your company address and phone number should be located on the homepage, and your team's photos with a brief job description should be easy to find. Don't overpopulate your site with text heavy content. The most important message to share is how your expertise will help solve clients' financial needs and wants.

- **Get on social media**. If you haven't joined the masses on social media, recognize that it is only a matter of time. Social media is an easy way to stay in touch with clients. LinkedIn, Twitter and Facebook are wonderful places to socialize, share information and find out about your clients' life events. Being regularly engaged with clients is critical to long-term relationships.

SHARPEN YOUR SKILLS

Any skill requires maintenance and ongoing development. You should never lose sight of the importance of improving your skills. Start improving your skills today by:

- **Revisiting and reacquainting yourself with basic selling skills and strategies**. Dig out old conference audios and books for a quick refresher.

- **Buying a new industry book**. Keep up-to-date on the latest strategies and techniques to inspire you to greater heights by grabbing a new industry book.

- **Listening to educational audio programs in your car**. Use the extra time in your car to listen to education audio programs to get updated on key industry news.

- **Attending industry conferences regularly**. Industry conferences give you the opportunity to network with professionals in your industry.

- **Providing technology training for your employees**. We recommend lynda.com, it provides a training tutorial for every imaginable technology application.

Many people get discouraged from taking small incremental steps because they don't see huge results immediately. However, those that stay dedicated and patient will stay abreast of their success for the long term. You can harness power in your business, with a little patience. If you take small strides every day in the areas outlined above, you will be on your way to making you an even more productive, successful and efficient professional than you were the day before.

You cannot achieve success by waiting for something to happen — you have to make it happen. Someone who is much smarter than me once said, "You don't succeed all at once and you don't fail suddenly."

Ask Yourself...

What small changes can I make today?

In my business life:

____

____

____

In my personal / spiritual life:

____

____

____

For my health:

____

____

____

You want the prospect to think of you first when their needs and expectations are not met by their current advisor.

CHAPTER 9

You Don't Always Have To Be #1

No matter if you are a seasoned advisor or new to the industry, nothing is more important than attracting a steady stream of prospects. Everyone in this business needs to be confident approaching people in their community to ensure the success of their practice. Having lasting relationships is part of running our business, but there's not just one single best technique to prospect. However, from my experience in the financial industry for more than 25 years, I have found if I can't be an immediate advisor, positioning myself as Advisor #2 leads to great success.

Advisor #2 is the one that is waiting on the sidelines when first place fumbles the ball. Many times, prospects are already working with an advisor, and when we are confronted with this situation, we tend to walk away or be impatient if we don't land their business. However, prospecting requires motivation, dedication and perseverance. Instead of giving up, get permission to stay in touch with them to help create a wedge between you and their advisor.

One way to effectively build a relationship with the prospect as Advisor #2 is to ask for permission to keep in contact. You could say "I'm really glad you are happy with your current advisor, but would it be OK to touch base at a later time with you, in case something changes?" Or, if the prospect tells you they are currently satisfied with their advisor, say "We are happy to be waiting in the wings and hope when the need arises, you will call us." Don't get discouraged if this happens, focus on providing value and nurturing the relationship. You must believe in the potential positive outcomes of your efforts.

To effectively prospect and stay connected, you must do your research and understand what they want, how they feel and what matters most to them. The attention you give and the way you correspond will help you stand out. (carla: please insert highlighted copy in a dialogue box also) You want the prospect to think of you first when their needs and expectations are not met by their current advisor.

There are many ways to help you get and keep your name in front of your desired prospects, such as:

- **Holding client appreciation events**: Invite your prospects to these get-togethers so they can see the great lengths you go to make your current clients happy.
- **Sending hard copy mailings**: Less and less businesses are using hardcopy mailings, the ones that do, get noticed. Stand out with hard copy newsletters, industry magazines, term rate sheets, handwritten cards, company flyers, postcards and handwritten cards.
- **Connecting through social media**: Social media platforms are an easy and cost-effective way to connect with prospects and provide an ideal environment in which to socialize, share information and provide insight. You will also have the opportunity to learn things about your prospect that will make for great conversation starters. Connect on LinkedIn, join groups that they are in and participate. Follow them on Twitter. Become an active voice by commenting, sharing or liking their posts.

- **Sending newsletters or email blasts**: Email is another cost effective way to reach prospects. It also provides instant access for prospects to learn about your company with embedded links to your website. This method allows you to know how your marketing efforts are working with email metrics. You can tell if they opened your emailed, clicked through to your website and what they did once they got there. Newsletters, industry updates, term rate sheets, blog, or even a general email message are all effective email prospecting methods.

- **Mailing thoughtful gifts**: Take your prospecting methods to a new level and really impress with books on finance, coffee for the office, restaurant gift cards and movie passes.

These strategies will slowly create a wedge between the prospect and their current advisor. Stay committed to nurturing the relationship and in consistent nurturing will open opportunities.

Recently I was in a position to find a new general insurance broker. There was no one waiting in the wings — no Advisor #2 for me to turn to. My theory on being Advisor #2 was solidified.

You are a sales person and your ability to grow your business is based on starting new relationships through prospecting. New relationships need to be nurtured, consistent nurturing will open opportunities. As well consistent nurturing proves that you are different from your peers who have given up. Effective prospecting can be predicted by numbers, that is, if you provide consistent value as Advisor #2 to 100 prospects, in 5 years how many will have become clients? What result would make your efforts worthwhile?

Regular client engagement strategies will have a direct and positive effect on your business.

Reasons To Diversify

Your Logo Here

Your Name Here
Your Address Here
Your City Here
Your Phone Number Here
Your Email Here

January

S	M	T	W	T	F	S
				1	2	3
4	5	6	7	8	9	10
11	12	13	14	15	16	17
18	19	20	21	22	23	24
25	26	27	28	29	30	31

February

S	M	T	W	T	F	S
1	2	3	4	5	6	7
8	9	10	11	12	13	14
15	16	17	18	19	20	21
22	23	24	25	26	27	28

March

S	M	T	W	T	F	S
1	2	3	4	5	6	7
8	9	10	11	12	13	14
15	16	17	18	19	20	21
22	23	24	25	26	27	28
29	30	31				

April

S	M	T	W	T	F	S
			1	2	3	4
5	6	7	8	9	10	11
12	13	14	15	16	17	18
19	20	21	22	23	24	25
26	27	28	29	30		

May

S	M	T	W	T	F	S
					1	2
3	4	5	6	7	8	9
10	11	12	13	14	15	16
17	18	19	20	21	22	23
24	25	26	27	28	29	30
31						

June

S	M	T	W	T	F	S
	1	2	3	4	5	6
7	8	9	10	11	12	13
14	15	16	17	18	19	20
21	22	23	24	25	26	27
28	29	30				

July

S	M	T	W	T	F	S
			1	2	3	4
5	6	7	8	9	10	11
12	13	14	15	16	17	18
19	20	21	22	23	24	25
26	27	28	29	30	31	

August

S	M	T	W	T	F	S
						1
2	3	4	5	6	7	8
9	10	11	12	13	14	15
16	17	18	19	20	21	22
23	24	25	26	27	28	29
30	31					

September

S	M	T	W	T	F	S
		1	2	3	4	5
6	7	8	9	10	11	12
13	14	15	16	17	18	19
20	21	22	23	24	25	26
27	28	29	30			

October

S	M	T	W	T	F	S
				1	2	3
4	5	6	7	8	9	10
11	12	13	14	15	16	17
18	19	20	21	22	23	24
25	26	27	28	29	30	31

November

S	M	T	W	T	F	S
1	2	3	4	5	6	7
8	9	10	11	12	13	14
15	16	17	18	19	20	21
22	23	24	25	26	27	28
29	30					

December

S	M	T	W	T	F	S
		1	2	3	4	5
6	7	8	9	10	11	12
13	14	15	16	17	18	19
20	21	22	23	24	25	26
27	28	29	30	31		

CHAPTER 10

Concept Calendars

According to Advertising Specialties Institute, 76% of people who received a promotional calendar had it prominently displayed in their home or office.

Your name and logo visible 365 days a year!

Since 1999, we have mailed calendars to our clients as a year-end client appreciation gift. However, today with the overload of new apps, devices and technology, we must admit we often thought about discontinuing the calendars. In this digital age we were concerned that our clients weren't using them, and opting to use the calendar on their phone or computer.

Instead of debating if they were or weren't, we turned to our clients to ask them. Through a survey we asked if they appreciated receiving our annual gift of a calendar. The response was a resounding "Yes!" We were thrilled to know they enjoyed getting the calendar, but we wondered if they were actually using it.

According to Advertising Specialties Institute, 76 percent of people who received a calendar have it displayed. Internet users are also still using paper calendars on a daily basis. This helped to confirm that our year-end gift was still effective. Not only is this the perfect gift, but it is also the perfect promotional piece. Your name will be prominently featured on the calendar and the unique concept images will draw others to ask your client/prospect, "Where did you get that?"

WHAT IS A CONCEPT CALENDAR?

A concept calendar is a traditional gift with a unique twist. The calendars we send to our clients are not a typical company desk or wall calendar. They are a laminated, 12 month, one-year-view, with a thought-provoking "financial concept illustration". Financial concept illustrations are creative and fun images that help communicate financial topics in a way that your clients will understand and remember. The calendars are also personalized with your company name and logo, which is clearly featured in the center. This means you will be visible to your client 365 days a year!

CAN I DO IT MYSELF?

Some of the best ideas are the simplest and creating these calendars falls into that category. We can provide the software for calendar templates, and all you need to do is insert your company logo and information, press print and laminate. You can even add magnets to the back to make it easy for your clients to display it on their fridge, all year long. These can be printed in your office with a color laser printer, or visit a local printing store for assistance. Make sure you have the calendars ready for distribution in mid-November.

To purchase the software, visit:
www.ideasforadvisors.com/easemarketingstore

WHAT ARE THE BENEFITS?

This is a highly visual marketing strategy that is not only useful, but also has the best return on your investment. They are low cost but high-impact. Surveys confirm that a functional business gift is crucial to its success. In addition to serving your client, the calendar provides an opportunity for discussion with friends and family. The concept illustrations will spark discussion, creating an opportunity for your clients to talk about you and your firm. They are simple to create and prove to be an excellent conversation starter.

Desk Calendars

Have an affinity to desk calendars? This past year we decided to try something different and order the traditional desk calendars. Our simple process gradually became very time-consuming. These tips may save your team time.

- Online choices are endless. We found that most companies are competitive. So don't waste time researching company after company. These two websites would be good choices:

  1) mynextpromo.ca
  2) 4imprint.com

- Expect to pay between: $2.00 – $5.00 / calendar

Let's see how this idea measures up to our *Marketing Strategy Criteria for Success*:

✔ Does the information establish you as a credible source?

- By giving a client a concept calendar, your kindness will be appreciated and referrals inevitable.

✔ Is it going to differentiate you from everyone else?

- These unique calendars will stand out from all other typical calendars because of the fun financial concept illustrations.

✔ Does it have high impact?

- The financial concept illustrations will stop people in their tracks and initiate conversations that will always go back to you.

✔ Does it have a long shelf life?

- 365 days a year! Amp up the advertising power by making a commitment to give the concept calendar as a gift to your prospects/clients every year.

Ask Yourself...

Is the Concept Calendar an investment or an expense?

It is an investment because it will be displayed which will keep me top of mind as well it is free advertising for me.

Will I print calendars myself or outsource?

___

Will all of my clients receive a calendar or certain segments?

___

Which month will I deliver the calendars? How much lead time do I need to complete this project?

___

___

The #1 reason clients leave is lack of contact from their advisor.

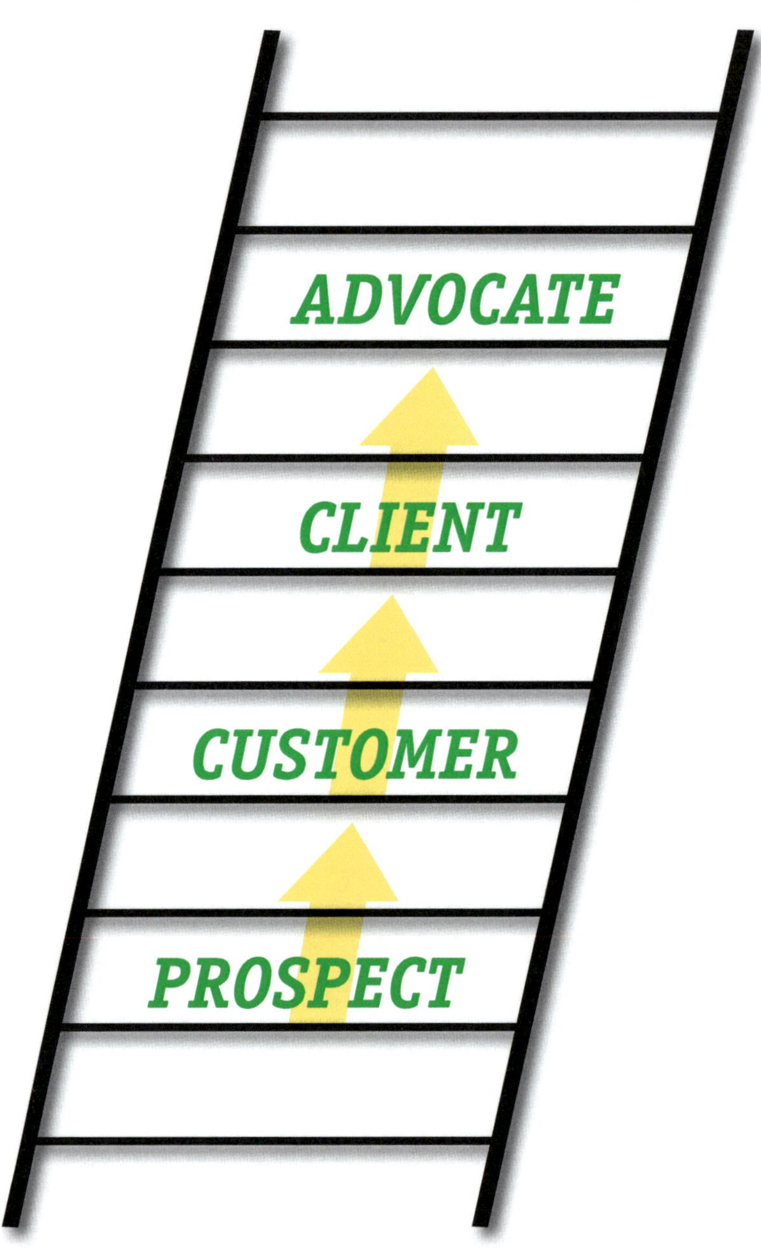
ADVOCATE
CLIENT
CUSTOMER
PROSPECT

CHAPTER 11

The Power of Client Retention

Whether you are a top producer or a less seasoned advisor, everyone has to develop relationships in order to keep their business thriving. Early in our careers, we are taught the power of graduating clients up the four levels of an advisor-client relationship. This is the process of developing a relationship with a prospect in hopes of getting them as a customer, then turning the customer into a loyal client, and lastly having the client become a desirable advocate. This is attainable to the motivated advisor, but it takes dedication, excellent client service and most importantly, regular client engagement.

CLIENT RETENTION RATE FORMULA:

Fostering loyalty through client engagement should be a systematic process built around your clients and the frequency that you feel is best. To begin, review your client list annually and do a year-to-year comparison to find out where you stand. You can do this by calculating your client retention rate and tracking your results from year to year. This will help you gauge how well you are executing your client engagement strategies and where improvement is needed.

Imagine you start the year with 200 clients. You then lose 20 clients, acquire 40 new ones and end the year with 220.

Clients Beginning of Year = 200
Clients Lost During Year = 20
Client Retention 90%

If during the year you attract 40 clients, that would be a 20% gain in the number of clients. However because you lost 10% of your clients you only have a net gain in new clients of 120%.

We could go much deeper here into the variables that grow your business but the key point of this chaper is to emphasize that retaining clients has a huge impact on your business over time. And we all know that it costs far less to retain a client then to attract a new client.

In my 25 years in the financial services business, I have found being regularly engaged with clients is the key to the success of creating long-term relationships. Incorporating even small improvements to your client engagement tactics can build and cultivate a mutually beneficial partnership, which will have a positive impact on your bottom line. The degree to which you either foster client relationships or not will affect your level of success; over the years we have adopted simple strategies that you can deploy into your practice.

CLIENT ENGAGEMENT STRATEGIES

From the very first meeting, you need to ensure your client knows they are a valued asset. Whether a person feels acknowledged and appreciated can influence their behavior. Cultivating the advisor-client relationship is at the core of what we as financial advisors do. Below are some tried-and-true strategies to implement today with your new or existing clients to show them you appreciation for their business, and your drive to go above and beyond.

Social Media

Using social media is an easy and cost-effective way to stay in touch with clients. These platforms provide the ideal environment to socialize, share information and provide insight. It's important to use your best judgment when communicating via these channels.

- **Facebook and Twitter:** These are the most popular ways to find out about clients' life events. You can become an active voice by commenting, sharing or liking their posts.

- **Blog:** This is a compelling communication tool that allows you to provide updates about significant events going on in your professional life. Sharing your blog with clients gives them insights into your business. Encouraging clients to share your blog is a great way to gain referrals.

- **LinkedIn:** Join groups that your clients are part of and that are of interest to you. Initiate conversations in these groups, and share your own insightful or useful postings.

Communication Notes

It's vitally important that you nurture your relationships and show your appreciation to clients through the valuable communication tools listed below.

- **Send a handwritten note:** This is a timeless and powerful gesture to show your gratitude for a recent meeting, referral or just because you were thinking of them. Consider a handwritten card for life events and holidays. For even more impact have your assistant put a thank-you card on the windshield of a client's car while he/she is in an appointment with you.

- **Text a thank-you:** After your meeting send a short and concise text that says "Thank you for the meeting" or even one to remind the client about an upcoming meeting.

- **Send an email:** This is a quick and easy way to send a post-meeting thank-you, and an ideal way to share recent product news and articles of interest.

Client Appreciation Gifts

Everyone enjoys being surprised with a gift to celebrate their birthday, retirement, wedding, or graduation. There are a variety of unique gifts that can help you score big with clients.

- **Create personalized stationery:** Have personalized note cards, sticky notes, letterheads, envelopes or pens created bearing your client's name. Clients can use these year-round, and each time they do they'll think of you.
- **Give a gift basket:** Create a lasting impression with wine, cheese and crackers, chocolates, coffee, tea, cookies, and other confectionary items.
- **Send a book:** You can send a book about personal finances to help your client better understand the financial planning process. Or, considering that most clients will have outside interests, you can send them a book about one of their hobbies.
- **Frame an autographed photo:** This may take some effort on your part, but your client will appreciate it. Find out what their favorite athlete or musician is, for example, and try to get a signed autograph that you can have framed.
- **Send a historic newspaper or magazine:** Find one from the day your client was born and send it as an authentic reminder of their special day. This collector's item is truly a one-of-a-kind gift.
- **Create "retirement business cards:"** This unique marketing tool gives the client's contact information and a brief (humorous) note about their schedule as a retiree. The cards will read "compliments of your firm or your name" in the lower right.

- **Make a charitable donation:** Find out if your client has a favorite worthy cause and make a donation. Then send them a card letting them know a donation was made in their name.
- **Develop annual custom calendars:** Create a laminated one-year-view calendar with a thought-provoking financial concept, personalized with your company name and logo.

Social Events

These events are implementable but require more time. Leveraging them will greatly improve your client retention, attract new clients, and more than likely increase your bottom line.

- **Office open house:** Invite clients and prospects to your office for lunch or after work. You can order food and even invite a local politician, sports figure or musician.
- **Client lunch or dinner:** Invite a client to lunch or dinner at one of their favorite restaurants or to a new hotspot.
- **Office lunch:** Surprise a client by delivering lunch for everyone in his or her office. Delivering it yourself is a great opportunity to prospect.
- **Tickets:** This may be a little more costly, but it will have an incredible impact. Invite your client to join you for an upcoming event, or give them a pair of tickets to a sporting event, concert, comedy show, play, ballet, etc.

IMPACT ON YOUR BUSINESS

Now is the optimal time to put these marketing strategies into action. Set yourself apart from the static in the industry by using these methods to attract new prospects, exceed your clients' service expectations and boost client loyalty. If you maintain an ongoing client appreciation program, you can maintain a steady stream of prospects and retain existing clients.

Ask Yourself...

What 5 things can I do right now to improve client retention?

1. ______________________________

2. ______________________________

3. ______________________________

4. ______________________________

5. ______________________________

It’s never too early
to start a conversation
with your clients
about life insurance.

CHAPTER 12

The Motivators for Life Insurance

In a market full of diverse financial tools, life Insurance continues to be a sought-after product for many reasons. Everyone has their own motivations for wanting to purchase life insurance, but it's up to you as the advisor to learn what those are. Understanding what motivates a person to buy life insurance will help you effectively develop a tailored plan for their needs, which can lead to a seamless sales process.

The most prominent reason people turn to life insurance is to fund expenses for loved ones who are left behind after a death. Love is typically always the top motivational factor that prompts people to purchase this product. People generally want to protect and provide for those they care about, whether it is their spouse, children, charity or church.

In my experience as a financial advisor, I have found that different stages in a person's life can influence his or her decision to purchase life insurance. The better you are at recognizing these life stages, the better you'll be at simplifying and clarifying any confusion, so they can achieve financial security and truly understand the value of life insurance.

LIFE STAGES

As people journey through life, they go through two distinct phases. During the first stage, they usually begin their career, make large purchases such as a home, a vehicle, etc., start a family, and save money. The second stage is when people are ending their profession, heading into retirement and planning for their legacy. Let's look more closely at how life insurance plays a key role in each life stage, and how you can help better inform your clients about this critical tool.

First Stage – Need It

This is the stage where people are beginning to build their net worth, perhaps start a family and make large purchases. Since their net worth is generally low at this time, they need life insurance for estate creation and security in case they die prematurely. However, people view the premiums as an expense but when bought at a younger age, a life insurance premium can be less expensive. It's important to educate your clients about this key information, so they are not intimidated by the cost. Remind them that life insurance is unlike any other investment—it is used to safeguard an income in order to prevent financial detriment for loved ones. During this stage, people want to make sure their loved ones are protected from financial hardship in the event of a premature death.

In summary, the key points of the first stage are:

- A perceived **need** for life insurance as **security and protection**
- Desire for **estate creation**
- **Premiums are** considered **an expense**

Second Stage – Want it

In the second stage, many people are starting to wind down and enter into retirement. This is when they begin to see the incredible investment element of life insurance, and turn to their financial advisor for guidance. Life insurance can be an effective tool to help clients financially plan for their passing by providing them with solutions for their family and estate. Also, with interest rates low for the past decade, many people are interested in looking at alternatives for their fixed-income assets. If you are building a relationship with a new client and his former financial or insurance professional had the foresight to put life insurance in place, you have the opportunity to explain how it has been providing both protection and investment in their financial portfolio.

In summary, the key points of the second stage are:

- People **want** life insurance to keep their accumulated wealth secure
- Desire for **estate preservation**
- **Premiums are** considered **an investment**

It's never too early to start a conversation with your clients about life insurance. No matter what life stage a person is in, there is a need for a discussion about this valuable tool. It is our role as advisors to guide our clients to make informed decisions based on their individual needs.

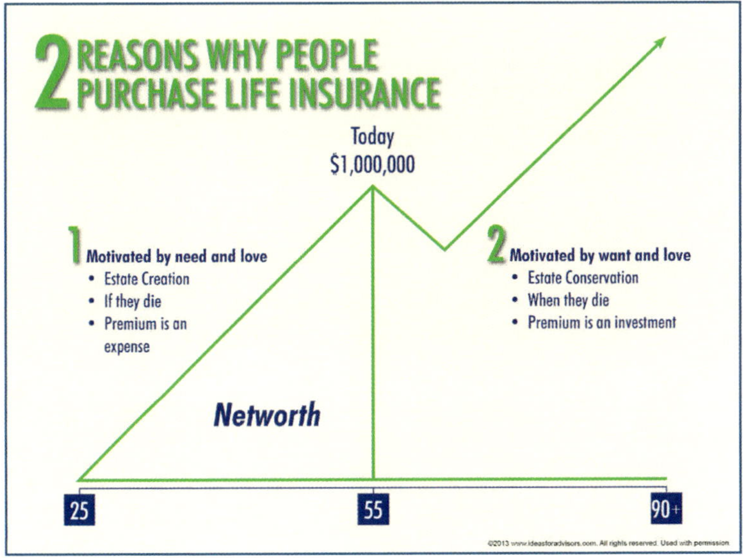

Notes

Being regularly engaged with clients is critical to creating long-term relationships.

APPENDIX

A Wealth of Resources

When it comes to personal finance, you are surrounded by a wealth of information. Sharing this information with clients is a great way to provide value and offer something extra.

BOOK LIBRARY

Build an office book library by ordering a selection of books that your clients would find interesting and would support the advice you give them. The book library should be accessible to clients. For example, in the waiting area or near your client meeting table/ desk. You could refer to a book during a meeting and then give it to a client on their way out of the meeting or you could mail a book as way to stay in touch or acknowledge a life event, e.g., graduation, retirement. Adding a personalized note inside the cover of the book would be a nice touch. Here are some of the books we have available in our office for our clients:

- *Paychecks and Playchecks: Retirement Solutions for Life,* Tom Hegna
- *The Millionaire Next Door,* Thomas Stanley and William Danko
- *The Ascent Of Money,* Niall Ferguson
- *Simple Wealth, Inevitable Wealth,* Nick Murray

- *Retirement Income Masters*, Tom Hegna
- *The Behavior Gap*, Carl Richards
- *Personal Finance For Dummies*, Eric Tyson
- *Never Too Late*, Gail Vaz-Oxlade
- *10 Ways To Stay Broke...Forever*, Laura McDonald and Susan Misner
- *Don't Worry, Retire Happy!* Tom Hegna
- *The Wealthy Barber Returns*, David Chilton
- *How Not To Move Back In With Your Parents*, Rob Carrick
- *Money Rules*, Gail Vaz-Oxlade

HELPFUL FINANCIAL WEBSITES FOR CLIENTS

These websites are a great resource for your clients. Share them with clients to support your advice.

- **www.gailvazoxlade.com** Well-known author and TV personality Gail Vaz-Oxlade teaches money management.

- **www.getsmarteraboutmoney.ca** This website will answer all of your money questions. Learn how to plan for life events. Also includes tools and calculators.

- **www.retirehappynow.com** Learn the three biggest reasons people run out of money during retirement. Tom Hegna will show you how to retire with guaranteed lifetime income and peace of mind.

- **www.lifehappens.org** A non-profit organization that provides valuable information and tools on life insurance, disability insurance, long-term care insurance and health insurance.

- **www.fcac.gc.ca** The Financial Consumer Agency of Canada is an independent body working to protect and inform consumers of financial products and services.

- **www.moneyindex.org/canada** This website provides the latest information from the top news sources and the most respected bloggers on the internet.

- **www.mint.com/canada** This free website will organize and categorize your spending for you. Pull all your financial accounts into one place. Set a budget and track goals.

WEBSITES FOR KIDS

Money education starts at home. Parents should start teaching their children how money works from an early age. Whether it is saving for new clothes or a trip to the candy store, children can learn very early about saving and spending. It is important because by the time they are teens their money habits are forming. These websites are great resources for families interested in teaching their children about money. This would make a great theme for a newsletter or you have a list of useful websites as a take-away in your waiting room.

- **www.themint.org** The Mint believes in educating children about money because the lessons on saving and debt need to be urgently learned. The site has sections tailor-made for kids, teens, parents, and teachers. The tools consist of games that are built around earning, saving, spending, and giving. Lessons on how money moves are also imparted in an easy to grasp language. With a basic understanding, you can play the quizzes and calculator games like the *Be Your Own Boss Challenge* on the website.

- **www.canlearn.ca** The Government of Canada website providing information on education savings and planning for post secondary.

- **www.yourmoney.cba.ca** An educational website for your children on budgeting, saving & investing, credit & borrowing.

- **http://life.familyeducation.com** Teach your child the value of saving and spending wisely. These games and tips will help him learn about the value of money.

SCHOLARSHIPS, LOANS, GRANTS AND AWARDS

Anyone who has gone through the process of applying for grants and scholarships understands the how complex and time consuming the task can be. This would be another great theme for a newsletter or have the websites printed as a take-away for clients.

- **www.studentawards.com** A free scholarship matching service, devoted to helping Canadian high school, college and university students by providing information about scholarships, bursaries, grants, fellowships and other financial assistance.
- **www.scholarshipscanada.com** Students can search for scholarships by name, school, field of study and scholarship provider.
- **www.bookmob.ca** This website is for post secondary students. Rent – Buy – Sell textbooks.

How to keep in touch with us:

Linkedin — Mike Morrow

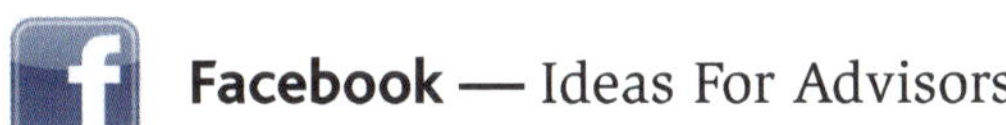
Facebook — Ideas For Advisors

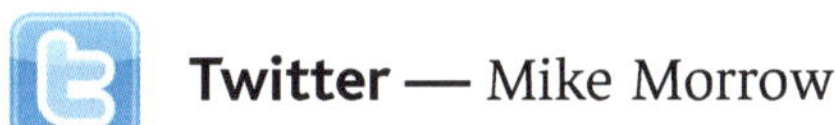
Twitter — Mike Morrow

YouTube — Ideasforadvisors

To book Mike for keynotes or workshops:
email michelle@ideasforadvisors.com

Made in the USA
Charleston, SC
30 April 2015